CW01214217

AN
ALTAR
OF TIDES

POEMS

Peter Ludwin

trail to table press
trailtotable.net

Copyright © 2024 Peter Ludwin

All rights reserved

This book may not be reproduced or transmitted in any form by any means, electronic or mechanical, including photocopying and recording, or by any information storage and retrieval system. Excerpts may not be reproduced, except when expressly permitted in writing by the author. Permission requests should be addressed to the author at peterludwin@live.com.

First Edition. Published by Trail to Table Press

Poetry
ISBN: 979-8-218-44698-7
Author Photo: Lisa Schmidt
Cover Photo: Natalie N., Pixabay
Cover Design: Jill McCabe Johnson

> Trail to Table Press
> an imprint of Wandering Aengus Press
> PO Box 334 Eastsound, WA 98245
> trailtotable.net

> Trail to Table Press seeks to publish literary works
> that transform our thinking about how we engage with the earth
> and each other as thoughtful, generous stewards in our actions
> and interactions, whether on the trail, as consumers and makers,
> or around the table through genuine connection and respect for life.

For Lisa

Contents

The Fastening Wood
- 2 | Digging Blackberry Brambles
- 3 | Hunger
- 4 | Girlfriend
- 5 | Corn
- 6 | Tools
- 7 | Earthworm
- 8 | Resurrection
- 9 | Remembering Theodore Roethke after a Return to the University of Washington
- 11 | *Swanson's Land of Flowers*
- 13 | A Reckoning
- 14 | Day Hike, Whidbey Island
- 15 | Makah Country, December
- 16 | The Bridge
- 18 | Kill Site
- 19 | Equine
- 20 | On a Landscape Job You Pour New Wine into Old Skins

Wind in the Rigging
- 22 | Pick Sticking Litter in a Park, I Come across an Abandoned Homeless Camp
- 23 | Planting Trees, Seattle, 1970
- 25 | Fresh Air Tavern, Seattle, 1973
- 27 | Aberdeen Fire
- 29 | Chevy Blazer
- 30 | Wayward
- 31 | A Convocation of Crows
- 33 | Watching You Sway up the Beach I Embrace an Altar of Tides
- 35 | Visiting a Nursery after Many Years Away
- 37 | Way of the Buffalo
- 39 | Earl
- 41 | The Journey of George Sitowahl
- 43 | Walking to Watmough Bay
- 45 | Morning in Forks, Olympic Peninsula
- 46 | The Promise

MIRAGE OF THE SNOWSHOE HARE

48 | Cherry Tree
49 | Awakening
51 | Showdown
53 | Medicine Crow
55 | Testing Ground
57 | Foreign Travel
58 | Investment
59 | Word Games
61 | Mask
62 | Do Not Disturb
63 | Reservoir
64 | Unforeseen
66 | Vienna, 1966
67 | Linc's
69 | To Decipher My Father's Cigarette Case
70 | Archetype
72 | The Book on My Father
73 | Arrow Flight

HAY ON THE DREAM FLOOR

76 | October, Tonasket
77 | Caretakers
78 | Opening Day
79 | Sleigh Ride, Okanogan Highlands
80 | Autumn, Okanogan County
81 | The Drive to White Swan, Yakama Reservation
82 | Fort Simcoe State Park
83 | Rural Red
84 | Driftwood
85 | Wolf Concerto
86 | Morning at Lake Leo
87 | On the Clearwater in Idaho
88 | That Country, That Time

Longing Buried in Stone

    90 | Imperative
    91 | Spirit Mound
    93 | Innocent
    94 | For the Instructor Who Told His Students They Could Never Write about the Moon
    96 | The Woman Who Stays
    97 | Rio Grande Gorge
    98 | Query
    100 | June 11, 1913
    102 | The Confession of Eric Brooks
    104 | Persistent Dream
    105 | The Bureau of Land Management

The Fastening Wood

Digging Blackberry Brambles

You know before you start this will be nasty,
what your neighbor would call *a real booger*.
Entrenched under thick, matted sod
or up against the side of the house, they defy
you with burls gnarled like a brawler's fist.
Trident roots splay down, then out to roam
as if loosed from all restraint beneath steps,
planks, the house itself. But when you leverage
the shovel just right, the snap, the muffled pop
of roots breaking apart conjures an older,
darker world: a mead hall cloaked in mist.
This must be the sound Grendel's sinews made
when Beowulf tore arm from shoulder socket,
omen of impending doom. And these roots—
this *is* to the death, is it not? Foretold when Adam bit?
A struggle borne on the season. One that's
just beginning. Sift the proof at your feet:
cottonwood fluff drifts to a snowy deck,
camellias litter the ground beside the sticky
residue of rhododendron husks, strawberries
cower beneath bracken ferns run riot.
Grendel? He wasn't coming back. Not like these.

Hunger

Up an abandoned Forest Service road to a logging spur
    with limbs that branch, then dwindle,
we climb the ridge rinsed by sporadic rain.
    Ground melted out yields snow
mated to grass and rock. Wherever we look we find
    scat, pellet-ringed proof of foraging
and bedding down. And on the dirt track, one small
    pile left by a carnivore, bits of teeth

and bone we can't name. Breaking into the open, we survey
    the higher wreckage—mountainsides stripped bare—
then the basin whose clear-cuts graze second and third growth.
    The primal forest long since converted
into panels, shingles, two-by-fours—board feet, the industry
    calls it. But we are searching for elk, or at least
an antler shed after the autumn rut. A sign, like the creeks
    and rain-swollen river carving the valley,

that a fragment untouched remains. True, we have two agates
    scored by orange zeolite we spied beyond a bend.
Other times that would suffice, but today we require more.
    And hiking cougar country
we nurse our hope that a shy, secretive cat
    will explode across the timber slash.
That, of course, doesn't happen. Nor do we chance upon elk
    until, back in the car, we turn onto the highway

for home. One crosses the road, and they appear: on either side
    a dozen calmly browse, the bulls' dark, shaggy
neck hair a leonine ruff. Cars in both directions,
    with no available shoulder, are slowing down
or stopped dead in their lane. No one wants to leave. *We need you,*
    we seem to be saying. *Don't go. Don't go.*
And they, lifting magnificent heads, show their rumps,
    slip like shadows through the trees.

Girlfriend

She places in the car, along with the viola
    for the quintet rehearsal,
a chain saw. She will need it to cut limbs
    trimmed from a windfall
by the creek where her mother lives.
    Her brother,
never dreaming she would one day earn
    a living from her instrument,
howled when their father coughed up
    the money to buy it.
In her back yard three cedar rounds
    inscribed by beetles
with a loping network of trails—
    a script evoking bardic runes,
Paleo-Indian hieroglyphs—
    await her hand.

I treasure wood, stone and words,
    she says, thinking
she should have been a carpenter,
    not a teacher
tied all day to kids and rules and bureaucrats
    who never seem to hear,
or if they do, merely turn and shrug.
    Better to listen to the silent
grain she knows lies just below the bark
    she chisels and strips.
To probe what the beetles have written,
    the poem
that defies linguistics
    to reveal,
when she peels the last band away,
    her laminate face.

Corn

Well past harvest season the leaves accuse.
Dried, dirty gray, they rattle with the wind,

hanks of hair to guard an Indian burial ground.
We've got to knock them over, Javier says,

so the soil can absorb the nutrients.
I begin with foot straight out—a kick, a shove—

but against thick or slippery stalks only angled
work will do. A martial artist in snowshoe boots,

I move down the fence line, fell them
with a single side-step rhythm,

the *crack!* a splintered bone. None remain
now save a small stand mid-field

that wields no defense.
I hack my way through—the boot a proxy

for a short sword, the feared Roman thrust—
then survey the fallen. Splayed askew,

leaves even more tattered in the muck,
these could be Custer's Seventh, the Alamo's

doomed defenders. A rain shower spreads
its damp voice. Whispers, *What have you done?*

Tools

Squatting by the coop where six baby chickens
scurry through a layer of wood shavings,
we hear a sudden *pop!*

It's the bamboo growing.

She knows the core of such things,
knows how to lash boards to the roof
of her car with open-ended ratchets,
how to choose the proper lumber for a deck
and make her Skilsaw cut a line drawn straight.

There's no one else to do it.

She doesn't mean it the way it seems,
though it hangs in the air like the smell
of burnt meat. She's right, of course.
The men in her family have always known
the *how* with greater instinct than the *why* of things,
wielding their myriad tools with the ease
of Wild Bill Hickok clearing Colts
from their holsters.

I think of the old Western actor Ben Johnson
in *Chisum,* rawhide tough,
telling her true-life relation John Wayne
he's had enough of his palaver about the bad guys,
enough of—you can almost hear him spit—
his goddamned *speechifyin',*
when it's high time he threw down.

All those pragmatic pioneers gouging their way
across the plains on wheels of banded iron.
And the poor, pathetic pen, a tool older
by far than the ones they carried,
moving with scarcely a sound through a night
lit by kerosene lantern, doing its best to keep up.

Earthworm

I bless the cedar in a clearing, chain saw angled
from my arm. The texture of its strip-smooth bark
shapes me as wind molds the clouds.
Yet who can say what plants this urge,
the current that shocks my veins to blue ice?
Always I have walked here as pilgrim,
hat in hand, my petition voiced in moss.
This time someone else. This time a logger,
1930, the tale of sap rising within loin and thigh
writ large in the rhythmic cut. No one foretold
that when the blade bit deep through outer
sheath to the pulp I would become the man
clearing his homestead land for crops.
Someone married to a bunkhouse in the woods,
my saw the driver of Weyerhaeuser's wealth. I feel
his forearm flex and torque when the old-growth
trunk—in this valley they were *all* old-growth then—
shudders, sways, then crashes to the forest floor.
Then praise the stump that will never grow anew.
Neither loss nor regret but a conquering pride
pricks the blood, the opponent felled
and ready to be bucked, choker-set, dragged
to the skidding track. I stand now as one,
brother to the hand raised against Abel.

Resurrection

Later, she would say there was no way to explain—
    not that it mattered—what compelled her
        to do it. After hours
playing quartets with friends, to head out alone

down an unexplored logging road, step with her
    viola into a clear-cut and accompany there
        a half dozen browsing elk. The piece she chose,
Borodin's *Nocturne*, caused them only to look up

from their forage, then lower their heads again,
    this music preferable to the raven croaks
        they knew by heart. But what began
as intimation, the contours of an ill-defined urge,

took shape the longer she bowed to the bow,
    a low moon rising fat between a bull's antlers
        the image that made it clear. Never mind
that his anxious snort drew the cows over a ridgeline,

their cotton hindquarters white flags of truce
    that vanished like hope. Here among stumps
        and slash she was performing, she understood
with each legato stroke, a sonata for hoof

and root. For that Lazarus chambered like a filbert
    within its shell who slowly rose from her tomb
        as if shocked back to unexpected life,
shroud ablaze at her feet.

Remembering Theodore Roethke after a Return to the University of Washington

—What's madness but nobility of soul at odds with circumstance?

A bear of a man, you were. A frown fixed
   as the bark of a Douglas fir grooved your face.
A scowl that signaled like a boil a gear internal
   was amiss—even as it belied the cadences

that propelled your words like driftwood.
   The reigning god of all who strove
to hallow language, in life you could whine,
   you could find fault. In the poems, never.

We didn't know the story: electric shock, the wild
   bi-polar rides you took at your amusement park
where water flowed uphill, then fled in ways
   no one could predict. But even if we had known

we wouldn't have cared. For us it was about rain
   that misted stanza, image, line. Soaked
the supple riot of bamboo, compost dizzied
   into floral displays whose fragrances

drove those devoid of nectar
   into their own dry soil to plumb
a vein or seam. If lucky, strike the core.
   From the Quad I stroll to the greenhouse

on lower campus where vines ascend in a humid,
   clammy tangle. This was always my link
to your world, vegetation rank and reaching,
   loam rich with rot. My hands, too, had pillaged

soil and root, labored under baskets draped
   in heliotrope and fuchsia flounce, encircled
pots molded green. Known the yoke of tactile,
   the drill imposed by hoe and trowel and rake.

In *The Lost Sun* I found the same aromas I'd inhaled
   doing that work: the odor of earthy desecration,
of geraniums on a bench. Scanning its lines,
   I absorbed wonder braided with wound.

This spring, digging up ferns to plant peonies,
   I observe buds strain to open, to ignite
the world. As with poems sometimes, I stake
   them to keep them upright in the wind.

Swanson's Land of Flowers

Old Milt mixed soil in the potting shed.
Shirtless, dirty, sweat gouging furrows as he shoveled
the rich loam. Smell of bark, of moist things
rotting. Binding skin like an oath.

It wasn't clammy, that shack. Not like the tropical greenhouse.
Nor fragrant the way heliotrope left me dizzy,
made me long for one of Gauguin's Polynesian girls.
This was of a different order: a blend
of sweat and stink and chipped wood,
the earth grained and sifted by air.

But mostly it was about Milt, his buzz cut,
the pale, streaked back, how he cursed
and smoked his drawn butts down.
And the dry laugh that told me
he always knew the score.

Maybe that's why I hung out there.
Gruffness straightforward as a pitchfork
its own good medicine. *This is a shit job*,
Milt spat. But he took pride in that shovel,
the territory it carved out.
Battered and covered with dirt,
like a boxer bleeding from a deep cut
above the eye, it retained a certain honor.

This afternoon, decades down the road,
I fill yard waste bags with pine needles
I've raked into soft hummocks,
clean muck and cones from the gutter.
It's easy to picture him then,

stripped to the waist in his shed.
The rattletrap mixer tumbles over and over.
He takes a last full drag on a butt. Crushes it with his foot.
Do it right, he says.

A Reckoning

> *God put those trees here for us to use!*
> —Forest Service Employee, Hyder, Alaska

As for our choice of trails near White River,
we take the wilder one choked with deadfall,
mud, the swampy bogs dotted by boardwalks

and cedar rounds laid in rows to ease our way.
Still, we call upon endowment to stay on point,
a skill to navigate winter blowdown and skirt

the chewed up black morass of drowned earth.
Ordained to halt before a massive fir whose bark,
a text to rival Moses' tablets, speaks its own moral law.

Knowing the fortune, the decisions made or shelved
that have kept it safe from the saw's unholy appetite,
we yield, we observe the silence it commands.

Comrades for a spell of the hollow-eyed owl
unmoving on his branch, ear tuned to a rustle
beneath the snow too faint for a man to hear.

Like a transfusion of blood, the trunk spurs
revival: transient, we know, but a nutrient
whose lack brittles mind as well as bone.

We've crawled under firs that block our path,
approached, then withdrawn from a skeleton
picked clean. Lessons written in moss and fern.

A script not taught but learned through the open palm.
It's taken this tree hundreds of years to tell its story.
Breathe in. Breathe out. Breathe in again.

Day Hike, Whidbey Island

    (for Joy)

On the prairie's far north side we strike
   the bluff trail, wind lush with salt,
with stories pried from kelp.

Or have we always owned their song?
   An eagle glides forty feet above,
wings held aloft without a quiver.

Dark as anthracite, it drifts toward terrain
   only it can occupy, more stunning
than even the lagoon trapped between beach

and bluff. Paused by a stark,
   sun-bleached log I see beyond you
the path it takes, the descent into myth,

a port I long to visit. No, not visit—
   recover. Fling my net over a dream
claimed as birthright, a child's first realm.

Baseball, fairy tales, hazelnut trees atop
   a wild ravine—all food to nourish
the living no less than a prodigal rain.

Like this bird's passive flight: such creatures
   open us like shells. What tide must
we invoke to cross the water?

Makah Country, December

This is where America begins.
This is where "America" ends,

our thirsty hope just that: to hear land
and water launch their own wild cry.

Hints along the Strait prepared us. The tiny
salmon port of Sekiu a raven grounded, no human

in sight. Now we stand where river meets tide.
Orcas, tribal as the sand our boots displace,

sometimes lance this boil as rain brackets
dreams of former whalers. Up the coast,

puffins front a cliff's gouged cavern.
Shaman beaks declare

they, too, have no need of history,
of flags that boast, *We own you.*

Conceits the elements erode,
convert to hammered dross, expel.

What sustains us here is wind,
what we crave begets the gnarled,

twisted branch. Keys that unlock.
That mottled shell splayed open, open…

The Bridge

>   (for Lisa)

For twenty-five years it's spanned the creek
that splits your mother's land, ever since
your father chain-sawed the cedar

that became the under beams, then laid
planks across. You used it to reach
the pasture, to learn the language

your horse whispered with her mane.
Now the center boards, ripped away
and piled to the side by your brother,

have rotted out. New ones in place,
he shows you where to drill the holes,
then pounds the first few spikes

into the fastening wood. How can I
prove myself worthy? Like your father,
who would sit in silence by a fire

and ponder a half-formed idea,
the nuts-and-bolts mechanics needed
to convert it into an object felt, inhaled, *real*,

your brother values most the concrete act:
an engine torn apart, repaired. So I swing
the sledgehammer he hands me,

drive spikes like some latter-day John Henry,
bent over to catch my breath,
while he grins to see his sister's lover stagger—

a man of words who knows nothing
about rotors, crankshafts, how to raise
from a bare foundation a structure

that will stand, will house and yes, *provide*—
stagger, then cleave again
the Indian summer air.

Kill Site

The skeleton my partner spots before I do
lies shadowed by conifers just off the trail.
Ribs arch up in parallel curves
from the ground—whether in protest
or supplication only elk gods can say.
Tiny flies scout the yellow bone.
Lack of antler screams *female*—
legs front and hind gone, too—while
the severed skull rests a few feet away.
Paired with rib ends gnawed, then notched.
Only a cougar could do this.
Near the two sets of remains a feathery coat—
the hide—smothers the earth.
Lisa gives a hushed assessment:

It must have been a terrific struggle.

I glance at branches overhead, their story
a breath withheld. The ambushing cat
had stalked a state park, a narrow strip
of old-growth forest wedged between
river and road. Beyond those boundaries
lies land mangled by machine.
Slopes stripped bare attest to brutality
of a different kind. Lulled by trees, moss,
the balm of water rushing or slowed to a trickle,
we'd embraced a realm benign.
Now death sinks like a stone.
Hovered above the spine, she takes its photo
but balks at shooting the skull.
Out of respect.

Equine

    (for K.)

After your father gave you the Arabian
you pastured for seven years across the creek
you often rode her beyond twilight,
a ticket into the night realm, into yourself.
Spirited in the manner of her kind,
she never walked a hill but, given free rein,
thundered up the slopes.
It thrilled you to command such power,
to direct with hand or knee
a creature who sped you from drama.
Those storms—unpredictable—that drenched
the toolshed, crops, whatever stood or moved
while drunken shouting tore the withers
of the world. Her gait,
like the cedar grove where the creek
tumbled toward the valley, was a definable
place, impervious as a Saxon shield wall.
Here you could wait out the sudden, blistering hail.

Not a little bewildered how a man
so fundamentally good, who came from dirt
and built the house he dreamed of
with his own life-wrecked hands
could bargain with a bloody moon.
But the horse, possessed perhaps
of a secret innate wisdom,
made no reply to your monologues,
vocal or silent, other than to turn for home
once the dark came down,
a blanket draped from cedar, maple, hemlock,
the furrowed bark of cottonwood and fir.
Sparks kicked up from stone
salved your wounds.
Points of light so brief, so fragile,
you snatched them like an owl.

On a Landscape Job You Pour New Wine into Old Skins

Out of a fable framed with willow and fiery
sword the Garden of Eden scribes fashioned

a fall, a future uncoiling like wire, scarred
by thorn, thistle, toil and woe, a crimson arc

splashed across the sky: the angel of death.
But today, wrestling with ivy in an old man's

yard, you feel sweat break along your brow
and think, *this* is paradise. This moist aroma

of decay from soil disturbed, the roots ripped
and rearranged that proclaim a common glory.

The strain of flesh, like the sound clippers
make as they sever multiple stems,

awakens the pores. With each clump
tossed in a plastic bucket you save yourself.

Again and again, the world. How is it
you are so blessed to turn toward your face

fingernails blackened with dirt? To struggle
with resistant vines? You stand to stretch

your back and a velvet-antlered buck appears.
Come, you say, let us break bread together.

WIND IN THE RIGGING

Pick Sticking Litter in a Park, I Come across an Abandoned Homeless Camp

A filigree of narrow trails begins
just behind the bathrooms. How had I
missed them before? Spread under a clump

of cedars, cheap carpets tell their stories
to an audience of bottles, cans, wrappers,
forks, fast food containers, torn bags,

condoms, needles, glass broken and scattered
as the people cleaned out of here a year ago.
Yells from a nearby playground

penetrate the brush I part with arm, leg, tool,
my steel-toed boot. A strained reach and *there*,
I grip another bottle. What bacteria continue

to thrive on the filthy mats, what hazards
they pose, don't matter. Because I'm
keeping score: *this* can gleaming from a thicket,

that Heinekens or Corona half-buried in leaves.
For hours I load my five-gallon bucket, haul it
out to garbage cans near the picnic shelter,

descend again into a faint gauze of menace.
Until, except for the mats, which a crew
will later remove, nothing remains to testify,

accuse, convict. As if a column of army ants
skittering away in the underbrush had come
through and devoured everything in its path,

leaving neither scrap nor trace, and around
the perimeter an angel armed with flame-
shooting sword held like iron to the earth.

Planting Trees, Seattle, 1970

On Fairview and Market and down in Rainier Valley
   we swung our picks that winter, sleet lacerating
      our faces, our hands. Blacks, Chicanos, hippies and Indians,

convicts larking on work release. Social outcasts all,
   digging wet, frigid holes with numbed fingers.
      Our ponchos angry crows that flapped and squawked,

danced and shook in the wind. It was a crew to love,
   that bunch. Gemini and Skinny Jim and John the Bahai,
      who played "Hoochie Coochie Man" on guitar.

And always, no matter how foul the weather,
   Pablo the Puerto Rican told crude locker room
      jokes most had outgrown by high school.

Taking whatever the storms threw at us, we only quit
   the day an avenging blast wrenched the hardhats
      from our heads and blew them far up the road.

That was forty years ago. I cannot drive by those trees,
   much larger now, without the ghostly shapes
      of that crew mottling the trunks like errant wisps

of fog, without a grinning, spacey Lamar erupting
   from a mock birthday cake somewhere on Capitol Hill,
      or Skinny Jim twirling his beads atop the post office wall

while my jug band showers tunes on a local street fair.
   Locked into the carefree early '70s before punk
      and disco engraved a headstone for the '60s.

The job lasted just a few months, the last gig
   coming on 45th and Wallingford when the sight of me
      stepping off an engineering department truck

in my Moroccan *djellaba* with a hard hat drew laughs and stares.
   The crew scattered into oblivion. They remain frozen
     in a languid pose the way a farewell photograph

of classmates shipping off to war, browned and softened
   with age, captures shadow from a charnel house.
     Illumines the graceless seeding of bones.

Fresh Air Tavern, Seattle, 1973

It was blues Valhalla, offspring of every juke joint,
    barrelhouse and Saturday night gin shack
        spawned by Southern field and lumber camp.
Couch a relic burned by countless cigarettes;

the bouncer, five-foot four, yanked from a motorcycle gang.
    On any given weekend you could hear *Black*,
        *y*ou'd feel your tongue smoke like griddle cakes
when Sugarcane Harris wove his demonic bow

or Muddy Waters scorched with Hound Dog Taylor
    and the House Rockers, the electric slide
        a sound to take your head off and hand it back
forever altered, down payment still owed.

But if you *really* craved the roots, ached for soil
    that steamed beneath an unforgiving sun, you caught
        Lightnin' Hopkins, asked Mance Lipscomb
to play "Goin' Down Slow" one more time.

That era, when you could ramble from the Fresh Air
    to the Encore Ballroom to hear Taj Mahal
        and four Afro-haired kids on tuba play the sweet,
syncopated marrow of cakewalk *funky*,

or slip into a Pike Street hole-in-the-wall,
    where Reverend Gary Davis—the *Rev!*—turned people
        inside out with "Death Don't Have No Mercy,"
engraved itself deep down, a scrimshaw on my bones.

They're vanished now, those old blues haunts.
    Shadows a dark, humid earth that spills
        from my guitar. Lost countries of the mind
shrouded in dust, in chords no longer played.

Gone like chain gang refugees from Georgia,
   from Angola, Huntsville, Parchman Farm.
     The boss man coiling and snapping his whip.
That tight-lipped shotgun rider.

Aberdeen Fire

When it scoured the Museum of History last week,
tail a monstrous black coil billowing skyward,
it swarmed the couch where Kurt Cobain slept in 1985.

But hell, that's Johnny-come-lately stuff. Back in the day
this was Wobbly country, ground that grew radicals like moss.
Those rough-edged, wild-eyed anarchist weirdos: mill hands

who'd lost fingers and entire arms to the saws, electrical
workers, shingle weavers, longshore—all manner of men
who spat, smoked, swore and fought, hitched up their pants

and went out on strike, 1912. Wages so low their sons
and daughters scavenged garbage cans behind the hotel
for old scraps of meat and bread, anything they could chew.

Aberdeen, gritty enough to rise from fire
that destroyed you in 1903, and during the Great War
another just as bad. Fire and rain, smokestacks and brothels,

a town so raw to the grain you spawned the king of grunge,
gorged on logs sawed and trimmed in dark, wet thickets
of limbs bucked to a tangle on the forest floor.

Who knew then you'd still be here over a century on,
a pugilist way past his prime, teeth knocked out or in,
flames trying to finish you off? But the ref won't stop

the fight. You're on the Encyclopedia of Forlorn Places
website, right up there with Butte, Detroit and all the other
towns gutted and hollowed out like cedar trunks chipped,

then burned to make canoes. No, the ref's got a bet down,
he's got a bet down, so the bell's going to ring for the 50th—
even the 100th—round, and when treasure hunters

with their picks and trowels and brushes descend here
thousands of years from now he'll grab the mic,
declare you the winner and still champ, cash in big.

Chevy Blazer

For years it sat rusting next to the Oldsmobile Intrigue,
her regular car sidelined now more often than not
in favor of a Ford Explorer because the Olds
had its own problems: a failed heater that defied
the best mechanics, a side window out, leaks.
And she never knew when it would just up and die
with no warning on freeway or bumpy country road.

A '75 with removable top, the Blazer
straddled the neighbor's yard, an eyesore
coated in neglect. She couldn't recall the last time
she turned the engine over, or even if it still
could start. Vague plans to get it running again
and sell it washed away with the rains. Truth was,
memory intervened. Like the time she parked

on a small dirt mound at the Indian fireworks,
the last spot left. Parabolas of exploding light
pierced the smoke, a tribute
to the roll-barred wagon that would go
anywhere she steered it: through creeks, woods,
potholes, ruts. So when a kid knocked on her door
one evening and said he had a thing for old Blazers

and wanted to buy it, she hedged. Sniffed around
the border of his desire. Knowing she should sell,
but seeing again those missiles when she was young
and, like the car, immune to lethal wrecks.
This machine that harbored no devious design
had never let her down, betrayed her trust.
I'll get back to you. And stepped again inside.

Wayward

Along Green River Road I just missed
    stepping on a flicker.
It lay near jettisoned cans of Bud

and Coors Light, not far from fireweed,
    from brambles
and a heavily timbered slope.

A male, the bird flashed black,
    white and orange,
with the telltale red gash

on either cheek. Even dead,
    it looked healthy.
Had it been struck by a car? A BB?

One by one I considered the possibilities.
    Maybe it had flown into a power line,
but that seemed remote. A life-gutting

avian illness? Death not from drama,
    but banal old age?
Any of the above, like theories

of global warming's impact
    on freak storms, might be in play.
Or could it be—flying over the massive

row house complex a developer
    threw up in a valley of diminishing woods
and produce farms—that its heart simply burst?

A Convocation of Crows

When I leave the house this morning
crows are looting the pumpkin field
across Green River. Nothing remains
of the corpulent gourds harvested

earlier this fall. But scavengers
can always find treasure
among the leavings,
coin in random scraps of straw.

I confess to a love affair with crows,
those carbon opportunists
eager to sell us our own dreams.
You have to respect a creature

so brazen he merits the snow petal
a showery gust pries loose,
reminds your tongue its home
lies downstream toward saltwater.

Not so long ago farms filled this valley.
Now the crows skim warehouses
and rows of corporate office buildings.
Split kingdom of the riverbanks

guarded by maple and giant alder,
thickets of blackberries at war
with upstart morning glory—this
is sanctuary, raw scripture of rain.

Driving past the pumpkin field
I listen to Coltrane blow silky gold,
his horn flared deep autumn.
Mt. Rainier rises, *sotto voce*,

above a gossamer layer of fog.
After a storm, prevailing winds spirit
the clouds east. What remains is new.
What shine are bramble and slug: pearl.

Watching You Sway up the Beach I Embrace an Altar of Tides

Such proportion befit a teenage girl,
    a roundness to offset the chop
of whitecaps when the wind came up,
    the sharp stones between tracks

and railroad ties we had to cross
    to reach the sand. A force
of nature like spruce, bullheads
    I caught in the shallows, the aroma

of kelp and sun and saltwater.
    You were the neighbor girl who fired
a blood already risen to heat.
    the older, unapproachable jewel

whose curves fell off the horizon.
    Was it then I began to love geometry?
Give arc and angle their due?
    I had a hunger for globes: those

that flaunted color-coded countries
    and fleshy spheres proclaiming riot:
a soft, fecund mathematics
    whose equations none could measure.

Movement at the land's receiving edge
    combined with shape to sculpt
desire's pain, its reeling churn.
    Dazzled by visuals, kinetics,

the hiss of spray and froth
    as gulls screeched overhead,
I entered a church only a boy
    could name. Nothing empty,

static. A music of motion advancing,
    then receding as opposites declared
two sides of the same moist coin,
    the same slippery word: *Alive*!

Visiting a Nursery after Many Years Away

The parking lot's about all that remains
as you remember it, but you can't imagine
Ted, the former owner, planting a row
of palm trees—*palm* trees!—as if smoggy
L.A. had invaded, then sickened Seattle.

The greenhouses face east-west now, the old
ones torn down for a classier, high-end look
or to make room for a café and pond of giant koi.
We don't propagate anymore, a young employee
explains. *It's really a garden center, not a nursery.*

You sense the ghost of Pearl Girl, unchallenged
mistress of the upper houses you watered at nineteen.
Long rows of fuchsia and begonia that beguiled,
while high above them

heliotrope draped from hanging baskets—
a siren with such heady, ripe perfume
you staggered under a vision of bashful fingers
peeling a woman's strap from her shoulder.

And where is Victor, the dirty-minded Dane who ruled
the tropical realm? Maybe that's why his thoughts
were so fetid, so coated with mold and green grime.
The potting shed, too, is gone, along with Milt,

though wandering a walkway lined with shrubs
you conjure his sweaty, half-naked frame,
the sardonic lip, the dangled cigarette as he shovels
and mixes, mixes and shovels, a stickpin to puncture

all illusions. Even the path that divided upper
from lower greenhouses, a vegetational Mason-Dixon
line, has disappeared. A fossil some scholar
armed with digital-coded imagery

may yet discover and submit for proof
these people once worked here. Their names
neither fact nor account, but in the resurrecting
manner of perennial, of hardy bulb—a benediction.

Way of the Buffalo

> *We're the people who believe in God, guns and Chevrolets!*
> —Speaker at a timber rally in Aberdeen, Washington

Fifty years since they closed the whorehouses down,
but when you walk the streets it could be yesterday.
Porno, pawn shop, tattoo parlor: the face

of a hard-assed lumber town whose chief export
is tough times, as much a given as the rain,
the soggy earth that rots men and boards.

On small treeless lots fixer-uppers bunch together
like nags put out to pasture, storm-wracked paint
a confession. Their silence a saw blade stilled.

Two decades past, the spotted owl watched over closing
mills and exports to Japan. Now signs sprout
like mushrooms along the Quinault River Valley:

Stop the 900-million-dollar Wild Olympics land grab!
The general store still sells *The Glory Days of Logging,*
and at The Hungry Bear Café near Sappho two crosscut

saws from years of high-stumping on springboards
adorn the walls like a crucifix. Devotional icons
whose clear-cuts leveled virgin forest to the Park line.

I'm a logger, growls a man in striped suspenders at the bar.
*I have a family to feed. You know how dangerous it is
to get your wood? Shit! Bring me another beer.*

Among piles of timber slash where foxglove thrives
and here on Aberdeen's streets you look for signs
of the old, ravaged faith. The atonal strain

that heralds termites at the foundation persuades you
it's no surprise this town whelped Kurt Cobain.
Spat him out to seek a grunge nirvana. No surprise

the orange crayon dream scrawled in disconnect
as water fell like swords among the wicked.
The seed blown far from the anchor chain.

Earl

ELVIS COOKS HERE. No way we could resist that sign.
Entering the coffeehouse, we climbed to the loft
and drank espresso near the bookcase
from which Hesse and Kazantzakis beckoned.
Why don't you bring your instruments in here? Blythe said
when we asked if we could rehearse on the patio,
and after each number people downstairs applauded,
even though we were just messing around.
But then Don piped up: *You boys sound pretty good,
and if you're passing back through here
we could probably book you in,*
and after we savored the bump that ante gave the pot
a woman named Kay kicked it to a whole other level—
*I thought you were a tape, I didn't know
you were actually* playing—*listen, I play the autoharp
and my husband plays guitar and we live
only a few miles up the road
and anytime you're in the area just drop in
and stay with us, don't bother calling
'cuz Earl never picks up the phone,
he figures if anyone wants to talk to him bad enough
they'll come on over and see him.*

We entered the ramshackle house
Earl had built on their acre near the ocean
and Earl himself came lumbering out from the kitchen
in boots that could crush a car, huge and burly
with arms like Oregon firs.
Earl, who arrived on his land with Kay and the kids
living in a school bus and worked construction
until the day he fell forty feet
off a roof and wrecked both ankles,
pain ever since a dagger.

Who fought Curtis when he bought the property
next door and leveled it so his kids could ride
around on their motorbikes,
then came on Earl's land, cutting trees
on a right-of-way strip he didn't want
before he built a sawmill in his backyard,
the saws screaming late into the night
until Kay couldn't take it anymore
and got the Planning Commission to stop him.

Earl, whose friend Paul took on the timber industry
because it was spraying poison
while cancer consumed the women
of Lincoln County, coming home one day
to find his house burned down
with all five kids inside.

Earl, who told a judge who threatened
to bulldoze part of his house
because it didn't conform to the building codes
that if he set foot on his property
he'd blow his damn fool head off,
who once threw a smoker out the door
because Earl thought cigarettes would kill him,
who liked to go crabbing and work on instruments
and had guitars and autoharps and mandolins
lying everywhere and kept chasing a rat
in the rafters with a stick.
Who one morning yelled in amazement,
Kay, there's a mushroom *growing in the shower*!

Earl, who sat down after we'd finished eating
and sang with Kay the most gentle, beautiful harmonies,
the notes lingering overhead long after we'd gone to sleep
like the tapping of rain
on the trees and the roof and the porch
and the soft earth around us.

The Journey of George Sitowahl

You were still young when the first whites arrived
and began to cut mammoth fir and cedar
a few miles to the north, skidding logs
down the steep hills of their town.
No eagle dove to clutch you in its talons,

nor did the rain that wove tribal tales in moss
miss its appointed rounds. As far back
as the Duwamish people could remember,
their river oxbowed across the delta,

its many rootlike fingers nursing eelgrass
strung along the saltwater shore. Salmon
probing its shelter for herring fed the village,
whose racks of smoke-dried coho and Chinook
flanked middens piled high with shellfish remains.

Growing to manhood, you watched the settlement
they called *Seattle* grow too until it bordered,
then swallowed your land. *We need to dredge
the river for our ships. Make it wide and straight.*

First to go were the eelgrass beds. That's when
the circling gulls—wary, disturbed—refused to touch
down. Then the delta succumbed to machines.
Was that why your bones began to leak their secrets
to the mud? The newcomers brought oil and metals,

a chemical brew where one day the storyteller
found the river god floating black and belly up.
By the time the stream that once scissored your sleep
had begun to kill off its wildlife, even the raven

had forgotten you—the last Duwamish to live
on its banks. Feeble, faint, you flailed the shack's
damp air. But arthritic fingers grasped neither
lamp nor shell. The coroner shrugged. He'd seen
this face before. Already given it a name: *starvation*.

Walking to Watmough Bay

Down through a long corridor of trees
    we pass
wearing a mantle of low clouds.
    Scattered by death,
yellow leaves decorate our hair.
    Today we transcend
our bodies. Today we inhabit,
    the wind
and lie naked with rock cliffs
    plunging to the bay.
Past their season, rosehip bushes
    do not acknowledge us.
But the darkening afternoon, the slate gray
    waters of the cove—
these speak in muffled voices.
    Tiny swells
undulate the blood.
    A flute
follows gulls into winter.
    Music for two fish
we play imperceptibly, feathers brushing stone.
    Within ourselves
we are shaping what the Earth
    spinning on its axis
shapes, we mold our own slow time.
    All points now
to a great shutting down of things,
    A flutter
of wings above a thin white candle
    burning
where the world unveils a minor key.

>   Isn't this
> what we decided lifetimes ago,
>   the touch
> of your rain-flecked hand
>   a witness?

Morning in Forks, Olympic Peninsula

A parting of curtains, a promise.
Smoke rises from a chimney down the street.
Across the roof, green patches
reveal squares of missing shakes,
and stumps in a neighbor's yard

announce the trees that once grew there.
Absence, from a clearcut slope
to the logging class they used to teach
at the high school, carries
more presence than what remains,

what's managed to survive.
The timber museum celebrates old-growth
they thought would never run out.
Now it has, and the crystal ball,
opaque as the cloud cover

trying to break up overhead,
lies tucked away in an attic.
One of those things you recall
you stashed with some boxes years ago,
but damned if you can remember where.

The Promise

I will lie down
with this old boat
in its grave and be glad,

a mansion for crabs
scuttling over my bones,
the dark silver of fish,

I will praise
the stones worn smooth
as thin soles of pilgrims

and weave a blanket of barnacles
at my loom in the half-open clamshell,
knuckles stippled in green.

The tide slapping
the worm-eaten hull will wake me.
Under a rising low quarter moon

I will dance a minuet of kelp
while gulls plunder gray waters.
I will face north,

a prisoner of thunderous trains,
and crawl beneath the curtain
of rain falling from my fingernails.

I will lie down,
this wind my protection,
the razor singing at my throat.

Mirage of the Snowshoe Hare

Cherry Tree

There was something about the sound of that branch
in a storm, how it lashed the window as rain
blurred and streaked the glass. An insistence:
bees swarming a meadow, a blood-song
hummed like wire at the temples.

And what could fire a boy more
in the womb of such fierce crackling,
that wounded agony of air,
than to read of capricious gods
while they let the Furies from their tether?

To cut loose like a bull rider
down pages of story and myth?
This branch was an omen I believed,
as when men of old in their anguish
cried out, *Lord, give me a sign*!

Water *could* pour from rock, rods change
to snakes and back to rods again. Words
as cut stones mortared into apse and nave,
transept and pillar. The vaulted dome
of imagination, one's private cathedral

that never reared the same face twice.

Awakening

I first truly fell in love with the world
when the Lone Ranger rode into my life,
so square he was cool—though not, I learned
later, as cool as Tonto, who wore buckskin

and melted into brush like a jackrabbit.
Still, the masked man galloped over the range
devoid of stain, speck, the errant smudge.
Not even a hint of sweat spoiled this illusion.

I was seven. Under a flowering dogwood
I pondered how to crack the code,
the hard, defiant nut.
What fueled the sweet pea staked to its frame

to snake far from its given course? Drove me,
a fledgling setting up his first ambush,
to snare the instant
a gladiolus broke the earth?

Could I freeze, to an infinitesimal tick,
motion's wheel? Wreck the gears of time?
And how to decipher a neighbor girl
twice my age who danced

around her cluttered room while light
filling the window swarmed her thighs?
The lust to cling to them as if to a spar
when a reef-wracked ship goes down?

Because it was all here in this lush, fecund hive,
the bloom of such riddles inhaled
as greedily as wind sanding my cheeks.
All here, yet veiled, and in that paradox

lay the spider's thread being spun,
weave and cross-weave, each segment a road,
a port of call, a gangplank choked with cargo
and crew from which a boat was always leaving.

Showdown

You would tell your son, if you had one,
about this trip you took when you were ten,
how old Highway 99 snaked past the Siskiyou Mountains
and drop-offs hundreds of feet down with no guardrails
for protection. That on the return from L.A.

his grandfather dared that stretch at night
ghosting though fog with only a blind sense
of where to turn the car—a tail-finned Lincoln—
while you gripped the back of your mother's seat
so hard the blood drained from your fingernails.

In Oregon rivers ran wild from rain.
You would describe that, too,
the Rogue pouring over the grille
as they waved you into Grants Pass,
the last car to make it, they said.

And reports of a locomotive washed away,
of people canoeing the streets of Corvallis,
how all anyone talked about was the rain,
the flood, the inconvenience of being stuck
in such a sorry-assed redneck lumber town.

You'd explain that you thought you understood,
but when the family saw *High Noon* everything changed.
That after watching Gary Cooper take out
the meanest-looking sonsuvbitches you could remember
while Tex Ritter sang

...Do not forsake me, o my darlin'

nothing mattered but the West itself,
the mythic and the real.
And he would nod his head *yes*,
but you'd know he hadn't gotten it.
Not really. Not where he *lived*.

Deep down where the silver bullet lies.

Medicine Crow

You remember winter on the river. The swarm
of crows storming cottonwoods along the bank

while the moon, gluttonous with light,
exhumes those secrets the fallow fields hold firm.

How anger drifting on the swollen flow
swirls back on itself, then snags a trunk submerged,

the incessant gurgle the revenge of a rain-soaked
season bruising the mouth. Mimicking men

on their porches, the birds argue among themselves.
It was better before they came, one says.

Then it was just the sun slanting through cedar.
That is the Indian crow. *No,* says another,

*it's much better now. Who leaves more garbage
for us to scavenge than these people?*

While they squabble you recall a different stream,
one from your youth, the father in hip waders

struggling against forces opposed to his design:
current, stones deadly slick, the steelhead he seeks.

Such a prize, that fish. It will elude him as he
eludes you, as the war so long ago continues

to lodge in a pool deep within him like bait
dragged by a lead sinker to drown.

No crows present that day the man strove to instruct
the son. And the boy—impatient—with no eyes

yet to see, no ears to hear as the man stumbles
and wades and casts again, bending to the task

at hand, cupping like a sun-blasted nomad rescued
by an oasis the water of his certain, delicious defeat.

Testing Ground

--Comes then the sudden turning back.
The mind, inverted like a fishhook, trawls its gray sea slick,
impales a loose shank of memory that flashes once before it's gone.

Out of Westport's early morning dark
   we stepped aboard the charter boat,
      my father and I, bound for salmon
   ten to twenty miles offshore.
All new for me, this riding out the pitch

when we hurtled down the steep green side
   of a trough, or worse, got slammed
      by swells that made us lurch like drunks
   across the deck. All new for a boy consumed
by books and baseball, the latter a divide

the Old Man couldn't bridge. We never lowered
   our rigs until, hours later, the waters finally calmed.
      I watched the captain bait my gear,
   club a fish someone else had caught. It flopped
on the slippery deck, then lay still,

a thin red streak trickling from its mouth.
   Riveted by the event, the blood that seconds
      before had propelled it to the lure, I trod
   the line that separates life from violent death,
grasped at some means to keep the fish,

but alive. A way, as yet unknowable, to soften
   shock, cushion the tender marrow.
      But the instant a coho struck my lure
   my own blood surged. I knew enough to arch
the rod, let it run, reel the impotent slack.

To play and coax it to the net, those eighteen pounds
 of silver we had canned in port. I knew enough,
  it seemed, to do what I must. I had what I wanted.
 The fish, yes, and dolphins off the bow.
And something more, something more.

Foreign Travel

Night. Out of a small green radio
the staccato voice of Leo Lassen,
baseball broadcaster, spins his rough
magic from the Pacific Coast League.
Seedy countries inhabit that voice,
places a boy can only travel in the mind.
No passport needed for pool halls,
flophouses, boxing smokers
and Skid Row gospel missions,
the thrill of illicit card games
played among sailors and squint-eyed hustlers
chewing fat cigars. Nor for street walkers
tattooed by rain,
the neon beacons of porn parlors.
Evoking Seattle's gritty realms
during a time when all that matters
are timber, fish, the planes that Boeing
builds, he lurks like shadow,
a foghorn beyond the slap of water.
Morphs as the game begins into shaman,
a gravelly weaver of *noir*
who needs neither feathers nor smoke,
chant nor invocation to take a boy
down Valhalla's royal road.
As for sacrifice, a timely bunt
to move a runner from first
to second base will do.
An act, like the voice, anointed.

Investment

Varnished with a luminous shellac, the best of the blonde
    tackle boxes opened to trays and rows of lures.
Here the iridescent plugs for bass, there flies and spinners,

trolling spoons for salmon, steelhead, rainbow
    and sea-run cutthroat trout. They meant for you,
Father, what art or coin collections mean for other men,

those luxury cars they acquire so they can say,
    This is who I am. Is it too much a leap
to regard those lures as portals to the closed

off rooms you tended, tarot cards of the secret
    inner man? I never told you how I loved
the leather-handled grip when I hoisted a heavy

box, nor how its weight matched the burden
    you bestowed the way rime, then ice slowly
suffocate a tall ship's rigging. How long it takes

a reefed sail to unfurl on its own, then stretch
    its canvas frame, stiffened by disuse
into a gelid slumber, remains as well the rainbow's

tale. Suspended for months like an emulsion
    claimed by winter, it stirs with the melt,
it begins to barrel toward the fly.

Word Games

Saturday nights we played Scrabble
and waged our private war in the dining room.
I stalked you there, my cunning a rival to those jaguars

you once hunted with arrow and bow.
As when a boy I tracked your past for clues,
scanned articles, a pilot's license, photo albums:

tilting—a doomed knight-errant—at windmills.
I used that stealth to bait you, to prowl
the board at will for huge scores

and set my traps in a jungle of perilous words.
Do you remember raising your eyebrows
in pain, honor affronted, the disgust

when you drew a rack full of vowels?
I knew I had you then. I'd box you out,
make a run like Fast Eddie Felson

in *The Hustler* ramming home every ball in sight.
I admit at times I felt bad I'd won because
I was brash and you were growing old,

a proud lion no longer able to keep hyenas at bay.
That's when the voice spoke up:
I'll pull some money together and take him

back to Vienna. We'll have coffee mit Schlag
and he'll show me the room where he was born.
He'll tell me about Brahms and how it was

under Franz Josef before the world blew up.
You refused—too much loss—but I knew
it nonetheless—this last attempt to connect,

to penetrate the layered curtains we'd erected
through words as I admired the cold dumb
tiles moving like a plague across the board.

Mask

On the wall between a jaguar and the Panchen Lama
    of Tibet, a photo of a Tuareg haunts. A monk
        spinning his prayer wheel begs him
to unwrap the cloth from his face, to reveal
    more than eyes framed by slits.

I huddle in collusion with the monk. My father
    the Tuareg, the night rider, the bolt
        of blue cloth wound tight around head,
heart, campfire, stories the desert steals.
    Out of many, just one. Fussing with fishing

tackle, the Tuareg. Watching *I Love Lucy*, a blue fog
    needled with spines. Coming off a business trip,
        boys to be seen, not heard. *Who was that masked man?*
The Lone Ranger, all right, always leaving, always riding away
    from people who rub eyes blinded by dust.

At twenty-five my brother asks the Tuareg
    to *really* tell him about his life.
        It's all in the albums, the Tuareg says,
and prods his camel back into the desert.
    No, that's not what I asked for—

But the sands have already swallowed any trace
    of the dark rider. A southbound train pinched
        between water and wooded bluffs rumbles on
while gulls screech their melancholy. Motion—
    of boxcars, clouds, waves, ships—laps against

the Tuareg's invisible armor, the quarterstaff's worn knob.
    Layers of sedimentary rock ground down by seas
        long since disappeared lie exposed to the geologist's
probe. Find the trilobite, face upturned. Pass the bone
    fragment. Don't stop until you turn blue.

Do Not Disturb

See him in his gold chair, age worn like an overcoat
    at once too heavy but needed to rebuke the cold.
        See the survivor, the father, the man.
The face wreathed in alpenglow, forefinger idly

tapping to a Schubertian rhythm—or is it Brahms?
    You don't recall, but what matters today
        is Viennese master as envoy from a past
imperial, regal, lost. A key to turn the lock.

It's a dream you realize he has earned. A furrowed
    scar's imprint on flesh, the mist numbing each
        psychic corner like gas on a battlefield,
confirm it. If he's caught up in the Fourth Symphony

or the Trout Quintet, why not let him wander there,
    far from bayonet charges into the teeth
        of machine guns, faces turned black, entrails
tangled in wire? You feel you could almost reach him

now. Find the door ajar. But when you think how crowds
    in Vienna, Paris, Berlin, St. Petersburg rode waves
        of mass euphoria as they cheered over and over again,
It's war! It's war! Thank God it's war at last!

you know he remembers it, too. And that even your palm
    drifting like down onto his shoulder
        would be too much, a gesture more invasive,
more severe, than a shell's florescent malice.

So you step away, arm still as a willow branch
    dulled by sultry weather, your voice a silent pool.
        You step away, bowed beneath a newfound burden.
For the first time, you defer. You let him be.

Reservoir

Faint, my father's track draws me to a restaurant
called the Hangar Inn next to a prop plane airstrip.
I find him, dead these forty years, in the Cessnas.

From childhood I've sought the hidden spring
that flowed only when the cock crowed once.
Even then its banks remained guarded by lions.

After eleven hours of flight training the old Empire
sent him up. The deep crease a machine gun slug
tore across his wrist, the crash near hostile Kurds—

gifts from a diplomat inhaling his cigarette.
There were others, darker and undreamed of,
when whole generations woke up screaming

at the viper in their midst. His physician father
blown by a mortar to chaff, the four brothers
scythed by similar storms of steel.

I have carried him within me like water
trickling through my fingers, wrestled the disease
his shadow cast beyond scrapbook and tackle box—

those tangible ores. I only wanted him to emerge,
a hunter from the forest. Just that.
Let the sun thaw the sluggish, stolen blood.

Reel in a startled voice, as if he himself had laid out
in a clearing a brightly colored parachute that shouted
to would-be rescuers: *Over here! Over here!*

Unforeseen

As if posed for a portrait, he occupies his favorite chair,
   his butter gold appendage. Suit, cufflinks, spotless tie:
my father looks the Protestant part. Yet religion

never marks him. From childhood a formal fit
   has been the thing to do on what people
in more pious times called "the day of rest."

Well, this is it, you think, introducing him to two hippies
   going home to Berkeley after picking apples up north.
This is it—and will the last man standing please close

the door behind him? Shabby clothes give you away,
   speak of field hand labor—"peasant work," aristocrats
in his old Vienna sneered through their lorgnettes.

As a boy watching the Emperor's carriage pass in review,
   he understood that this world of caparisoned horses,
of sash and saber and epaulet, the blinding elegance

even his native language prescribed in the second person
   singular, was immutable, a natural wonder like Orion's
starry belt. He lay in bed then on his back, arms folded

over his chest the way the Jesuits had drilled into their
   charges, knowing with cultivated pride that Jews
and servants had their place somewhere beneath him.

Courtesy, ingrained since birth, drapes him like a cloak.
   His soft hands, the moons of manicured fingernails,
a statement. The same hand that fingered a bullet

wound just above the wrist parted the thinning hair,
   smacked the bald dome of his forehead when surprised.
He doesn't do that now. Limping toward you, the hip

a permanent wound, he extends the hand gloved
   in story, greets your barbarian friends.
And what do you gentlemen do?

Vienna, 1966

A cloudbank shrouds the Ringstrasse.
Nothing can dispel its mood—
not the Prater's giant Ferris wheel,
the Riesling savored over dinner,
the caricature of a stock Viennese waiter

whose flaming shish-kebab lights his passage
as he navigates the quirky angles and sawdust floor
of the Griechenbeisl—the "Greek Joint."
Nor the Summer Palace where you entered
this world, Father, on a great swirl of Baroque.

Before I leave I'll buy a torte at the Hotel Sacher.
Send it across the sea. A token from the grim city
you fled five years after the War.
But today I roam the streets for threads, traces, torn tongues.
Mouths flayed by June 28, 1914.

In the Prater the band stopped playing
while a sword no one noticed began its slow descent.
A corpse in Sarajevo, a jerkwater town in the Balkans.
Patrons yawned, the music resumed. *It's only the Archduke.*
From his grave Mozart stirred: *Out of tune!*

In your day consumption ravaged the Viennese slums.
That's how this feels. A place still so shell-shocked
it's never moved beyond 1918, when the guns
at last fell silent and ravens complained
about the sudden lack of bodies.

A lacuna that marked your walled off retreat,
those steppes so immune to harvest.
The ravens would understand.
Bloated on ruins of family, of Empire,
they lost the power of flight.

Linc's

Check the small boxes for corkies,
spin-glows, jigheads, barrel swivels.

And over here, bobbers, squid jigs,
boogie bait. A sign in this small,

bare bones tackle shop admonishes:
Don't forget your worms and maggots.

After 67 years the owners, Japanese
whose long memories include a relative

packed off to Minidoka internment camp
till war's end, are closing its doors for good.

I imagine you, Father, rummaging
through such arcane gear, as I used to

see you pick among dry flies and wet
that filled trays in a cork-lined box.

The singing reel, the spoon a-flutter
in the current just before a strike

meant many things: sport, passion, refuge.
Your lone temple of intimacy.

I pause before a map display to savor
syllables of the former Indian world:

*Quillayute, Kalama, Wynooche, Willapa,
Washougal, Skokomish, Hamma Hamma, Calawah.*

The lush, liquid vowels, the sheer abundance
of sound so different from your terse tongue.

Mounted above, two Chinook salmon
over fifty pounds, one caught down in the bay.

That would never happen now. Did you ever
come here? If not, you should have.

This place reeks of Old Seattle,
that rough-edged town of bums and booze

along Skid Row. And the Kalakala ferry,
silver hull aimed for distant islands.

More at home with fish than family,
you wore the mantle of winter sleet.

That's why I've made this trip.
Before the finality of padlocks,

to feel you roam these aisles
while rain pounds the roof,

watch you test and flick a rod,
a set hook the only prize you seek.

To Decipher My Father's Cigarette Case

All those years I watched it open and close,
cigarettes bound like prisoners in gold bands.

I never thought to ask what lay behind the fleur-de-lis,
the signatures abutting symbol and precious stone.

Mistresses borne across the ocean in your pocket?
Heavy silver in hand, I recognize only your initials,

the blunt Masonic triangle. No voice from beyond
the grave tells how to root out the snowshoe hare

from its burrow. The insignias imply *aristocrat*,
those privileged titles America made you discard.

The case bristles with encrusted coats-of-arms, crowns,
Indian head coins from the 1850s, the weight

of a history buried. The meaning of the boar
on a Swedish medallion, the blood red Austrian

figure, escapes me. A lammergeier, I circle
for the rock that will break the bone

I drop, yield the marrow I need to survive.
At this moment a different food sustains me:

Howlin' Wolf. For you, a Viennese with a coffined past,
he'd be a riddle, a cuneiform slab that invoked

the dark side of the moon. But when he sings
about his little red rooster, about a spoonful,

I hear black earth fertilized by storms so violent
the chains dug up by harrows deny their very rust.

Archetype

(for Leonard Ludwin)

As for you, my minotaur,
I've tried augury, divination,
means ancient and new. Must I kill

to break the spell you cast? To swallow
life-saving fluid the cactus yields?
Winter has strangled my voice.

The maze: A murder of crows
drives me inside. Clew of twine
held fast—a lifelong habit—

I raise a torch fashioned from rags and pitch.
My mind sees beyond oxygen-starve flame,
its sputter syncopated along the wall

until it reveals something that resembles you,
a shadow I graze with my finger.
Soft and wet, no snarl nor beastly features.

And eyes that implore, that demand a ticket home.

Where are the horns, the fearsome claws
that have always haunted my sleep?
Stumbling on a rock slick with excrement,

I lunge to save the torch jarred from my grip.
Stench envelopes me, a death cloud
makes me gag. Dizzy, I wonder:

What if I lay myself down between rocks
and old bones? Gave up a skin rouged
by thorns? But my sword hugs its scabbard.

Urgent now, I drag you to open air.
Who claims the minotaur? a voice
calls out. I do. The chimera already grows cold.

But where is the proof, the severed head?
On my tongue, I answer. On my tongue,
wrapped in cloud cover. A precious stone.

The Book on My Father

So many blurred or empty pages, their margins
twin posts of a barbed wire fence.
This story, like the loon's, begins and ends in mist.

In between, the lake still as glass, obsidian waters
that never reveal their secrets. And spectacles
that incarnadine the sky like Goya's brush—

don't they serve a dual purpose: to enchant, distract?
Who, after all, can resist liquid drunk from fable?
An Indian head, soon to be shrunk, on the jungle floor?

Or Mongols raising curved swords, a last-second
reprieve, prophecy, disguise, escape,
coincidence that defies, then compels, belief?

All the while, a kayak drifts toward the far shore.
Nine-tenths of an iceberg hides beneath the surface.
Only when it melts does it reveal itself.

But even this is mirage, dimension with no visible shape.
Go ahead. Dip your oar, your paddle.
Watch the water run down, run off, run away.

Arrow Flight

Those old Germanic tribes knew how to do it right.
As a boy you read about the dead hero
whose companions carried his body to the beach,
placed it on a boat with his armor,
torched it and set it adrift.
Then they straggled back up the sand,
got roaring drunk around a bonfire
and stayed the night telling stories of their comrade.
By morning all was ashes: thane,
boat, fire, the silent tongues of warriors
    veiled in sleep.

When they burned you, Father, they removed you shrouded
from the hospital, stole along crumbling, graffiti-scarred walls
    like lepers
whose ravaged shadows fell misshapen on the cobblestones.
You couldn't see their eyes drain the blood
from dark rivers, couldn't hear the jackal's bark
when they tossed the ashes like an old, broken-spring
clock that lacked even the memory of leaves.
Bearing you on no shield except the tarnished plate
of indifference, they filled out their forms.

No one raised a glass.
No one knew a story to tell.

None saw, in the bandit's storm of dust,
a gazelle outrun mirage.

Hay on the Dream Floor

October, Tonasket

To rise in the dark of the cabin,
bones shot through with cold
implacable as iron,
to stuff paper and kindling
in the wood stove, then run outside

to piss while your teeth rattled
like rusty chains hauled across a foredeck—
that was the beginning of apple picking.
It was a process, this slow
unfolding into day,

one sealed with pain that followed
you up the weather-beaten ladder,
clung to the hand you used
to grip a Winesap coated with ice.
Not religious, you prayed then for sun

to break over the ridge top
and find that hand, that fruit,
to fashion that deliverance
you knew was bound to come,
once you'd made yourself worthy.

Caretakers

These old barns
lean into the storm like buffalo.

Wind between their ribs
taunts the root cellar,

snow scatters
voices in the rafters.

Wooden skeletons
speak of who is not,

who once pitched hay
on the dream floor

when tears stained the fence.
Someone here milked desire

while the cow wandered off,
someone told stories to the snake.

Mildewed, they cling to planks
rotted away by whispers:

There is a time
and a time
and a time...

Touch the broken boards
and those stories blaze up like rosehips

igniting the Chesaw Road,
singe your fingers like frost.

Opening Day

This morning I stalk autumn aspen shiver,
land to hold me fast: a quilt.
Rifle fire across the valley barks at odds

with my roost on Little Whiskey Mountain.
Apple season almost done now, frost and ice
a daily shroud the earth struggles to cast off

while geese in V-formation flock south.

Orchards stripped of living fruit flaunt remains:
windfall, props, the bruised onset of rot.
Wary, a spiked buck eases

from a nearby copse. Silhouetted
against the sky, he stands for seconds
long drawn out ordained, not even nose

aquiver. The rifles echo, here less

nuisance than a fly. Then a bound,
and where an instant before he challenged
the trigger finger, a blaze of blue.

Sleigh Ride at Havilah, Okanogan Highlands

Havilah. A biblical word that means "land of gold."
The early settlers must have been thinking
about these fields in autumn,

how they rolled
toward not just the hills,
but a kingdom of plowshares burned down
the curved length of axe handles

and stamped on their homesteader tongues like leather.
Or aspens quaking along the soul's green
verge, a place where, given
the right conditions, any seed might thrive.

Tonight the gold lies buried. This horse knows all
about such treasure. He draws me through it,
through the lost cabin
built blindfolded before birth.

Across an upland lacquered with light
only the moon asserts a claim.
As for the rest of us,
we must summon the bird that flies backward,

we must augur with lanterns of straw.
Snow flown to the frozen traces stings my face awake.
The runners hiss like arrows.

Autumn, Okanogan County

Along Hungry Hollow Road aspens tremble with insouciance.
    Rosehips the size of ball bearings, the Highlands'
signature fruit, trumpet their sanguinary blaze.
    Once they were just flavoring for tea.
Now each fleshy globe teems
    with a separate life I've led.

Past Havilah an overlook beckons, the gulf below
    bounded by slate blue ridges
that summon the hollow bone, the slanted wing within.
    Here even the buzz of a horsefly has value,
a freshly minted currency. Poured like silver
    on the air, it makes a prisoner of sleep.

This land of rifle and harrow, of skinning knife
    and men seared by weather and frail
margin clings to the tongue like dust.
    What I've known best of the Okanogan
has been this season, this golden dying
    that makes the pony stamp his brief history

into earth as salmon go flush at the mouth.
    Under the crush of winter snows
most of the barns built by pioneers have sagged,
    then gently surrendered.
But even new ones with metal roofs defer
    to the old music at night.

This is a forgotten world.
You must pay to take it with you.

The Drive to White Swan, Yakama Reservation

    (for Allen Braden)

I remember how that road ran straight as a rail
twenty miles west from Toppenish,
each sight

along the way a signpost fleshing out a life.
The hop fields first, nets
and angled posts

a skein of webs strung to catch
cones the female bears.
Then bales of hay

stacked for winter feed, irrigation pipes scattered
among a patchwork quilt of sagebrush,
yards and grassland,

junked cars left to bleach and rust
as porch pumpkins grinned
a trick-or-treat tale.

It was impossible, passing those corrals,
not to conjure Tonto's
faded tracks,

wonder what trail the Lone Ranger now rode.
By the time we reached
White Swan,

too small to warrant even a token traffic light,
the Indian rider we saw coming in
had disappeared.

Fort Simcoe State Park

    (for Allen Braden)

The sweet smell of the pine board blockhouse
    belies the stink of horse and mule,
        the sweaty men who soldiered here
    when the tension of a bent back bow
nocked with arrows could lie like heat

over the valley. Not that it did much.
    The Northwest tribes were small.
        Where are the Cayuse, the Chinook, today?
    And the Yakama in White Swan, a one-stop
dot on the reservation map, will salute you

with beery smiles, cans upraised like pipes:
    homage to the four directions.
        Relics now the stately commandant's quarters,
    the plain rough planks that housed enlisted men.
Outlasted by Garry oaks that tower

a hundred feet above ground, their canopy
    a shield against the sun.
        That star, like winter cold,
    the sole blade to still scar the land.
Favor a blossoming wound.

Rural Red

Trump for President signs color code highway 97.
No trace of Dems in cattle country, where a man
at a roadside stand slivers buffalo jerky to nibble.

Lie low, watch your topknot, keep your powder dry.

We've come to the mountains for larch,
the one conifer that gilds evergreen slopes each fall.
But cottonwoods along the Cle Elum River

drown them out, their brilliance cut from a band saw.
Five miles up a dirt Forest Service track,
beyond tiny Liberty with its back-in-the-day

ore carts, rock samples, pioneer wood stoves,
five wild turkeys waddle, peck, waddle again.
Their single hard note call pierces more than air,

an arrow that snaps a pine branch, cleaves along the grain.

Rooted, we cast our votes, declare our party of choice.
As the turkeys amble over a low rise their exit
frames a politics of wind, of mist that begins to part…

Driftwood

      (for Lisa)

Burnished smooth by water
   into a snag the color of oiled flesh,
of a palomino bronzed against a barn,

it needed your hand to pluck it
   from the river. Maybe tamarack,
you reasoned, from the wood's heady fragrance.

A piece like bristlecone pine,
   though you were hundreds of miles
north of the windswept Sierra Nevada.

It came from the Teanaway,
   the same valley where three bull elk
with racks to match browsed to the sudden

braking of cars on our return from Montana.
   For years it lay on your living room rug,
lovely but almost an afterthought

until you moved it to a table
   draped with a blood red shawl:
Guatemala's dark weave.

Even before dawn, when a gull heralds
   the arrival of onshore rain, it glistens.
Swears through luster alone that,

as you pinch between thumb and finger
   an agate fished from the shallows,
you draw the curtain from light.

Wolf Concerto

Let it begin with the fish. A scrum of spawning
    pink salmon massed at the head of Silver Spring.
      Let it begin with them—the living, the dead,
the dying stressed for air, the yet unborn.
    The full cycle, the wheel's unbroken arm.

Sing me a song of drift. A phrase of light corralled.
    Track the path they gild across the mountains.
      A drier land, this. Needled by upcountry pines.
Along the North Fork Teanaway River, swaths of fur
    that once clothed a browser bear ragged witness

as heat pencils my wrist. No carcass or scattered bone
    in sight. But cradled somewhere in the valley,
      canis lupus, gone nearly a hundred years—
poisoned, shot, trapped out—has come back. Begun
    to leave his mark on tree and bush, his howl

a streak that binds the moon. Hunter, myth,
    he pads to a noiseless gait, a shadow
      at play in the mind. See the elk snared by a starry
flume bed down for the night. A scent. Unfamiliar.
    How, nostrils flared, he turns to test the wind.

Morning at Lake Leo

Last night's frogs and bats and tree-scaling moon
    not forgotten, we slip down

the path to the water. We've packed up the tent,
    stuffed ground pads, sleeping bags,

the folded breakaway poles in their sacks. Ready
    for the road, but not yet. Mist still peels

off the lake
    while sunlight filters through,

the yellow-flowered lily pads—impressionistic—
    spread in clumps offshore.

Then, a bonus: two otters chuffing
    like bellows, their territory breached.

Intrigued by these long-legged aliens, they look,
    dive, swim, emerge, stare again,

their routine an arabesque, a damp shower of leaves.
    As if for them, too,

the world itself is unfolding, has imbued the panels
    of a stain-glass window

with a flush, blood-swollen light until they fuse
    and melt. The space left behind

the province now of a raven newly fledged,
    amazed at the empire it rules.

On the Clearwater in Idaho

She insists we stop. A river means rocks,
stones worn olive-smooth and scored by thin
ribbons of rust. Candidates for the windowsill

at home next to a bird nest remnant the cat
has not destroyed. We're supposed to meet
a woman in Moscow, but already Lisa's out

of the car and picking her way along the bank,
a heron stabbing the shallows for food.
I join her, grudgingly at first,

eyes alert for color: for copper, Sicilian green,
white's blank chastity. I'm on the hunt now,
wading in the river guide Chaco sandals

I wore when I drove shuttle on the Rio Grande.
Near a brush clump I pluck a stone—andalusite—
as if it's a rare aquatic fruit, a prize I bring her

like an offering, a shank of sheep a Hebrew priest
would have laid upon an altar for his God,
then set afire amid spit and pop, a burst

of scalding grease to make him cover
his face in fright. A short way off a family
pans for gold. Nothing to fear on this stream

but rattlesnakes the canyon breeds like pinecones.
What God may be lies in the details. A mineral shine
embalmed in wetness, the language of Lisa's eye.

That Country, That Time

It was a sky hard as chert
when the geese told their story.
It was sorrow on the mountain.
A forlorn honk misting the tamaracks
and pony breath near the aspen grove.
It was hunger driving the wild, fevered eye,
frost joy the magpie called its own.
It was the groan of the apple bin,
a harvest that fed my resurrection.
It was squashes and raw cider
for sale along the river,
the dregs I chewed like barley, thinking *nomad*.
It was storms I inhaled before their arrival,
barns crippled and strapped for deliverance.
It was rosehips and a lost flame kindled,
it was charcoal in the bone.

It was sauna and snowbank and a pale moon talking.
It was dream cloud and cabin as rosin
flaked from the bow.
It was the dancer spinning far off-center,
the bare branch wind-whipped by tears.
It was the hole buried in night song,
the blackbird who never came down.

It was a promise
a beveled thorn

and always
always

it was the heart
the insatiable heart of it.

Longing Buried in Stone

Imperative

Set to leave Illinois for the West, she finds
the wagon so full it holds no room,

not even for a humble iron. But she's off
to the Promised Land, and it's going, too.

Tied to her waist, it dangles between her legs,
Batters and bruises the gaunt, weary flesh

across Iowa, Nebraska, high, dry Wyoming.
When her husband becomes too sick to walk

she pushes him in a handcart, the iron
swinging with each step, each bump in the trail.

Wolves have already dug up the graves of cholera
dead left behind with clocks and portmanteaus.

Months of heat, hail, wind and bugs bend her back
as she staggers into Salt Lake. Now, steam

rising from her laundry toward a sky so empty
all her sins evaporate like rainwater, she holds

the iron aloft. She has invaded country
claimed by Kansa, Pawnee, Cheyenne, Arapaho,

Bannock, Shoshone, Ute. With hand callused
and hardened, weather-beaten as a shack

of clapboard siding angled away
from an incessant prairie wind,

she wields a weapon, a tool to brand.
One by one smooths the damp wrinkles.

Spirit Mound

Begin with the naming of things.
"Prairie," from French via the Vulgar Latin
prataria and further back to the Latin *partum*,
meaning "meadow." And the mound itself,
called by geologists a *roche mountonêe*—
a bedrock knob carved by the last Pleistocene glacier.

But long before these names, known to the Omaha,
Oto and Yankton Lakota as Paha Wakan,
an evil place inhabited by humans
eighteen inches high.
Who, according to legend,
killed anyone in range
with tiny arrows.

Then profile the prairie itself: tall
rather than short-grass, and a century
after pioneers ground it under for corn
whisper a word gashed by their plow:
"ecosystem," from the Greek *oikos*: house.
This then is the house I wander, this small island
with roots up to nine feet down dwarfed by a cultivated sea,

each plant a single room
in which the naming practice blossoms.
Here grow bluestem and sideoats grama.
Wild bergamot. Ox-eye and milk-vetch.
The gray-headed coneflower. Cordgrass. Indian grass.
Goldenrod and *panicum virgatum*.

When I reach the top I bite
into my apple and face west.
Isn't that what Lewis and Clark did
when they climbed this hill of Niobrara chalk?
West. Where the sun kindles rebirth.
Like this site seeded, then restored
to what the explorers saw
on their walk through Dakota country.

Except for the wound that won't close.
From the mound they counted
more than 800 buffalo and elk.
This morning *bison bison* is missing.
Vanished from the *oikos*.
The house whose door,
hung from a rusty hinge,
clatters against its frame.

Innocent

Not the Cheyenne woman still asleep
    after dawn ignites the prairie,
        she who once welcomed alcohol's
    searing burn as totem, a spirit power
to which even wolves would grovel.

Not the foster parents who raised her
    to be a pale stem of corn without roots,
        lacking the very soil to nourish them.
    Nor the brother who asks you, a white
stranger, to move your car so he can leave

not just the yard but your foul,
    contaminating presence. Not even
        the stream along the property line
    that contains the sullied memory of blood,
the splash of rigid bodies. Who, then?

Perhaps these buffalo grasses a breeze
    fans back and forth as if they were women,
        naked as the earth, weaving a primal dance.
    You turn and walk through them toward
the stream. This grass that for thousands

of years fed the great herds. So different,
    you muse, from those uniform rows of wheat
        your own people imposed on the plains.
    The light this morning reveals by blinding.
You see painted men on horseback. Members

of the Bowstring Society riding south
    to attack the Kiowa years before the stream
        showed a crimson face. They won't return.
    All around you the whisper of waving stalks.
Those with no stake in the game.

For the Instructor Who Told His Students They Could Never Write about the Moon

1) Homestead on the Texas Plains, 1840

    Summer, and you've learned to dread
    that ascending night light. Transfixed
    by its swollen belly, you listen,
    ears cocked like a rabbit. Your stock
    is fenced, but what's a fence to *them*?
    A twig to snap before the knife blade,
    fire-heated, carves its cruel song.
    You knew this when you pushed west
    beyond the settlements, but like the bison
    you had to migrate, impelled by a deep,
    unseen river you never managed to name.
    Now light floods the room. You toss
    and turn on your cot. Hoofbeats
    pervade these plank walls.
    And when you search the window,
    a lance, a shield, a face painted black.

2) Sand Hills, Western Nebraska, 1910

You don't recall a past life in Texas.
Don't know why the moon tugs you
like the tide. This evening, a predator
in ambush, you lie on a low rise
and wait for cranes. But you carry
no weapon. Just your aging eye.
What would your father have thought?
If somethin' moves, son, shoot the sumbitch!
Their cry like no other, the cranes
stir your sluggish blood. One more trip.
That's why you look up tonight.
A pair skims the silver disc,
their course a plume of smoke adrift.
Remnant from a grass fire.
If only you had a gift to make words
sing, you think, you would write a poem.

The Woman Who Stays: Flathead Lake, Montana

The words will do it.
Not the body singing its sad tune
off pitch, nor house décor:
tribal rugs artfully placed
among dieffenbachia and vines,

mandala hubcaps nailed to the walls.
She will like them well enough,
as she would embrace mesquite
or the pensive steal of fog
across a tide pool crushed with longing.

But without the words they are nothing.

Because she knows the lies poets tell
are the very seeds of moon shadow,
of anvil and chrysalis, stasis
and the river
that flows back to its source.

The deeper truth of the sun
burning a hole in the mirror
is the cry of the one-eyed night bird
as it sweeps down through the trees.
She will hear the clouds groan

before they break apart.

Rio Grande Gorge

If Coronado, dazzled beyond repair
by rumor, by legends tended
more fiercely than any mortal crop,

had taken the Low Road to Taos in October,
he would have found gold, all right,
gone blind from surfeit of it,

the cottonwoods on either side
extracting tribute from his eyes.
And once, driving through a storm

east of Albuquerque, I watched
a cloud transform from vapor
roiled at random to a buffalo,

then an Indian pointing north.
A rainbow spanned a horizon
so savage, so black I spun off

into *cante jondo,* Lorca's deep song
steeped in blood and shattered glass.
Into a past composed of absence,

of adobe weathered and crumbling,
helmets rusted out beneath the yucca.
Conquistador, you should have known

that in a land of angel fire
alchemy has many practitioners.
Spittle and clay once made a man see.

Query

       (for Garland Oral Ethel)

In the Highlands the old barns talk, their swaybacked
   posture a language already archaic, curiosa from a book.
      Even the names settlers gave their locales—
Chesaw, Havilah—sound out of time, seeds dropped
   to fend for themselves against thistle, drought,

the virus of dust. Of just plain neglect. When we met
   you were long gone from the Okanogan country,
      fled from gritty circumstance. A place
defined by calluses and gutted deer hung from a limb.
   But a newspaper from the buckboard era

revealed your father, wanted by the law. Everyone
   knew this land charged double for those
      who hadn't first made their peace.
That Jim Ethel was one of those dangerous boys
   some women inhale like cocaine.

A scholar, you fell from a different tree. The stoop
  of your rawboned frame as you broke down
     Chaucer's lines freezes like Winesaps in October.
Teeth beginning to stain crowd your mouth, voice reedy
   yet resonant, as if at birth grains of wind-borne

pollen assailed the sinuses, a wayward gene that lodged
   there. So I have to ask you, Garland, if the feral
      snarl of Jim Ethel, trailed to the cabin
where he holed up with 200 rounds before the posse
   burned both to ash, caught an updraft.

If it blew, like the memory of his blackened body,
   across decades of silence to make you finger
      your long-neglected gun. The gun you used
.to shoot your wife, her terrified sister and husband.
   Then turn on yourself.

Striding through the same room you poured sherry,
   past all the books, past the Knight, the Miller,
     the Wife of Bath: Milton's flawed satanic angel
spitting fire and smoke. I once picked rosehips
   along the Chesaw road. Flew in a horse-drawn

sleigh toward Mt. Bonaparte, moon a swollen gourd.
   Recited Chaucer just to hear my tongue roll.
     Maybe you lost the rhythm of this land
I came to embrace, its cadence, its quirky grammar.
   Forgot how to parse the barns.

June 11, 1913

    (for Jim Ethel)

The morning after the posse burned your cabin down
  they raked out the bones. Your son, the sole family
member who lingered close by once the shooting started,
  stepped forward over charred, still smoking timbers
to identify the skull. His fingers rimmed the two
  bullet holes, self-inflicted, blown through the temple.

Wouldn't you agree it's not far-fetched to draw a line,
  to say with sound reason one could predict
such a demise long before you dynamited
  John Hones' boiler twice? A boy
who cuts off a teacher's ear, then shoots
  him through the leg, drinks from a different cup.

And who can say, coming home many years before
  on the heels of an Apache uprising, what seeds
took root when you found your first wife's body
  pinned by a stake to the ground? No wind could
erase the tracks that led to a man holed up behind
  a false partition with two hundred rounds.

As for your son, asleep in a bell tower to finish school,
  not many in your pioneer county turn Communist,
however briefly, or become one of Plato's darlings.
  Those few seized by literature rather than cattle,
by philosophy, erstwhile queen of the sciences,
  instead of deer season, the latest apple prices.

Knowing how your rages rose to darken the sky,
  he refused to fault the posse. Fifty-five
rode to bring you in, some of them friends,
  but you swore you'd never go back to jail.
In his book-lined house over sherry
  he stoked my hunger, fueled my thirst,

a catalyst when I lay open and dry like tinder.
　A scholar, he pointed me to the rarest
of minted coin. Until the day, eighty years old,
　he killed his wife, then shot himself. Like you
only during fire season when flames outrace men
　at the hoses, then turn on a gust to engulf them.

The Confession of Eric Brooks

So here he stands hidden in the autumn
   of a high drainage, frost not yet thawed,
     a clearing where he sees the bull advance,

the branched, sky-raking rack a spectacle to pinch
   his breath as he sights through the Springfield's scope
     to the killing zone just behind and a bit below

the shoulder. Recalling in that moment
   the five-point antler he found the previous fall
     athwart the trail, one of its tines a chipped,

scarred testament to combat. No way to know
   who won, he or a rival bull, or if he'd survived
     the winter. He might have starved, or a cougar

could have snapped his neck from ambush. Then again,
   this could be that horn's former owner, the bull
     who now stops, surveys land and creek, the chill

morning air, before its head swings toward the man.
   The body, unmoving, facing still the cherished
     broadside angle the hunter wants. Habit holds

his rifle frozen to the shoulder crook, curls his finger
   in the trigger's welcome hollow. The rhythm
     of a ritual so often practiced as to be unconscious.

Mon-tan-a, a raven croaks. The man's blunt,
   defining syllables a creed, a code burned
     beneath flesh and bone to the pith.

Yet, he hesitates. Later, in the saloon he and his friends
   call home, the one dotted with the land's wild bounty—
     mounted heads of deer, elk, moose, bighorn,

bears both black and grizzled—he will find it difficult
   to explain how at the instant an errant slant
      of light fixed his gaze, fusing it with the bull elk's

own, his arms began to lower, his breath and the breath
  of his quarry billowing forth in clouds
     of fugitive vapor.

Persistent Dream

    (for Janet)

Of all the shelters people contrive
   for themselves on the border—
buses, yurts, trailers, caves,

the crumbling, reconstructed ruins—
   your one-room *ranchera* house
was always my favorite.

The two stone columns Manuel built
   in the grip of a cocaine habit
create illusion, like the desert itself

and the lives of people we knew.
   Each winter when I arrived
from the north I marveled

at your lush vegetation: outsized
   greasewood, ocotillo that spiraled
like El Greco's figures toward God-drunk

reunion, the ghostly blue gray candelilla.
   Walking the shrine trails that wove
through that wild garden, I craved an Eden

of my own. Whenever a storm turned
   the mountains dark, greasewood savaged
by wind, my roots grew ever more tenacious.

Until death emptied that house.
   Until, after a raven flew down the arroyo,
the greasewood itself stopped waving.

The Bureau of Land Management

    (for Janet Sullivan)

It returns: your sarcastic Louisiana drawl
whenever we spoke of the BLM,
how that accent planted a defiant flag:

The Bureau of Livestock and M-i-i-i-nes.
Driving this afternoon through BLM land
I mimic that sound, the first step on a path

to reconciliation lined not with stone,
but matches coming one by one to flame.
Where you thought hippies

could do no wrong, I saw caterpillars
trapped by their own spin, a revolving door
too often shrouded in smoke. You condemned

the Border Patrol, I thought they had
an impossible job. For nine winters
we argued in this vein, you who chucked

an insurance business for the badlands,
and I with one foot there, yet long removed
from the stoners' rose-tinged carousel.

During a misunderstanding
we allowed to fester like the proud,
heated flesh around a sliver, you sent a letter

I left for months unopened, afraid to find
in your words a sharpened file.
Only after a phone call

told me a series of strokes had claimed you
did I perceive amid the settling dust
the bond had not snapped. I've never gone back.

Others have died or moved away. I could endure that.
Not your absence. I don't want to hear coyotes
mourn. Feel the wind toss you like a rag.

Acknowledgments

Grateful acknowledgment is given to the editors of the following journals in which these poems first appeared, sometimes in slightly different versions.

Cirque:
    Girlfriend
    Earthworm
    Linc's

Common Ground Review:
    A Reckoning
    Awakening
    Caretakers
    Opening Day
    Morning at Lake Leo

The Comstock Review:
    Reservoir
    Wolf Concerto (Winner of the 2016 Muriel Craft Bailey Memorial Award)

Concho River Review:
    Sleigh Ride at Havilah, Okanogan Highlands

Connecticut River Review:
    Do Not Disturb (2017 Pushcart Prize nominee)

Crab Orchard Review:
    Rio Grande Gorge

Flint Hills Review:
    Swanson's Land of Flowers

Floyd County Moonshine:
    Chevy Blazer
    Driftwood

Front Range:
    Morning in Forks, Olympic Peninsula

The Hurricane Review:
    Foreign Travel
    Testing Ground

I-70 Review:
    Kill Site
    To Decipher My Father's Cigarette Case

Kansas City Voices:
    Pick Sticking Litter in a Park, I Come across an Abandoned Homeless Camp

Mad Poets Review:
    The Woman Who Stays: Flathead Lake, Montana

The Main Street Rag:
    Mask

The Mochila Review:
    Watching You Sway up the Beach I Embrace an Altar of Tides

Naugatuck River Review:
    Planting Trees, Seattle, 1970

North American Review:
    Spirit Mound

Off the Coast:
    That Country, That Time

Oyez Review:
    The Journey of George Sitowahl

The Pacific Review:
    Showdown
    October, Tonasket

Pinyon:
    Hunger
    Tools

Pirene's Fountain:
    Archetype

Plainsongs:
>Innocent

Poem:
>Digging Blackberry Brambles
>Corn
>Resurrection (Second Prize Winner of the 2016 Paulann Petersen Poetry Awards)
>The Bridge
>Wayward
>Unforeseen
>Fort Simcoe State Park
>The Confession of Eric Brooks

Quiet Diamonds:
>Day Hike, Whidbey Island (Finalist for the 2020 Malovrh-Fenlon Poetry Prize)
>Fresh Air Tavern, 1973, Seattle
>Aberdeen Fire
>Visiting a Nursery after Many Years Away

The Raven Chronicles:
>Earl
>Medicine Crow

Red Rock Review:
>Equine
>June 11, 1913

River Oak Review:
>Query

Samisdat:
>Word Games

San Pedro River Review:
>Arrow Flight

Sin Fronteras/Writers without Borders:
>The Book on My Father
>On the Clearwater in Idaho

Slant:
> Remembering Theodore Roethke after a Return to the
>> University of Washington
> Way of the Buffalo
> Investment
> Vienna, 1966
> Imperative

Soundings Review:
> On a Landscape Job You Pour New Wine into Old Skins
> A Convocation of Crows (Reader's Choice Award Winner,
>> spring/summer, 2016)
> Cherry Tree

South Dakota Review:
> Autumn, Okanogan County

The Texas Review:
> The Bureau of Land Management

Weber: The Contemporary West:
> For the Instructor Who Told His Students They Could
>> Never Write about the Moon

Windblown:
> Makah Country, December
> The Drive to White Swan, Yakama Reservation

The Paradigm Poets Anthology:
> The Promise
> Walking to Watmough Bay

"Walking to Watmough Bay" also appeared in Vol. 2 of the *Aeolian Harp Series Anthology*.